Serendipity Empire

OrangeBooks Publication

Smriti Nagar, Bhilai, Chhattisgarh - 490020

Website: **www.orangebooks.in**

© Copyright, 2023, Author

All rights reserved. No part of this book may be reproduced, stored in a retrieval system, or transmitted, in any form by any means, electronic, mechanical, magnetic, optical, chemical, manual, photocopying, recording or otherwise, without the prior written consent of its writer.

First Edition, 2023
ISBN: 978-93-5621-491-0

Serendipity Empire

PART 1: The SuCcesS

ASHWIN KRISHNA VIJAY

OrangeBooks Publication
www.orangebooks.in

Contents

1) Introduction   1

2) The Beginning Of A Start   3

3) The Welcoming Of The Call Made   10

4) Realities Recreating   18

5) From Nowhere To Now Here   51

6) The End Of A Beginning   64

7) O-A-K, A-A-K   74

Introduction

Welcome to the illustrated incident of a life. This story provides seat to fasten up your belt along with sense of success. The unfolds you are about to make will let you understand the story with extreme satisfaction and curiosity. This story is about an icon in the textile industry, my life and ultimately in our story. He is the man who failed losses and won profits. Now we are about to engage our consciousness with the story, but before that, I would like to thank the individuals who gave me permission to include the names and those who have been brave enough to let me use their testimonies.

Obviously, this is how I have seen things. It's my personal perception of events and others may have seen them differently. Some of the events and incidents are edited to safeguard few communal phases and social prestige, but my intention is simply to give your true feel for what was his life about.

I want to say a very special thank you to **Mr.Revanth sir** and **Mr. Arun Raj sir** who were the causes of this effective book. Also I want to thank **Mr. Maria Austin Diaz sir** who helped me to increase my literacy level. Especially I am grateful and much thankful to **Frontline**

Millennium School and it's management team **(Principal Mrs.Lavanya mam, Co-ordinator Mrs.Arul Nikitha mam, Mr.Rathis sir, Mr.Nikil sir, Mr.Veera Selvam sir, Mr.Rajasekar sir, Mr.Prabhagaran sir, Mrs.Selvi mam, Mr.Andrew Alexis sir, Mrs.Nazareth Mary mam, Mrs.Ruby mam, Mrs.Rabia Begum mam, Mrs.Nirmala mam and Mrs.Kalaiyamuthu mam)** which tirelessly worked with me by providing the best faculties to update the first edition of this book (incomplete one) into the version you read today.

I am now 16, born 2007. That was the main reason for publishing this book in a late period of time. I was not matured enough to publish this book globally because I was not able to approach the proper publishing protocols and other required sources. But now I am an author. This is due to the iconic man, whom we are about to read.

The Beginning Of A Start

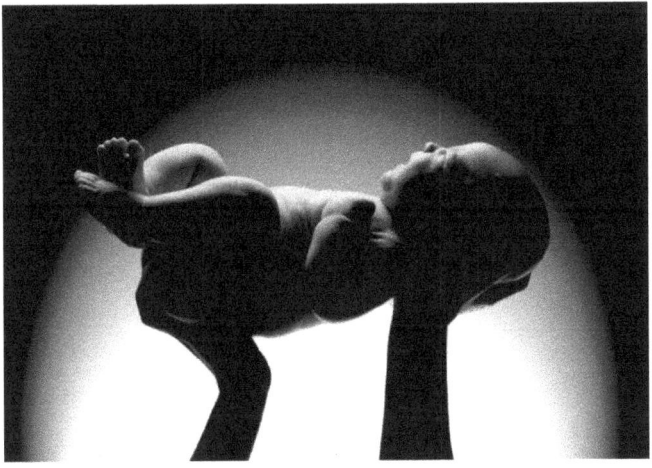

In the year 1973, May 5th, a history was born for the sake of victory and Success. He was the sixth and youngest son in his family. He was grown up by hearing words from his parents "You are born for a huge reason because the first three babies were dead soon after their birth and you are the sixth & the youngest child in our family. God has brought you here for a reason. You're blessed." He enjoyed his childhood as everyone does. His family was economically weak but had high honor and prestige over the village people. He was the first child to go school and learn things. By years getting passed away, he realized his poverty. So he studied well and passed grade 10. By then, due to the extreme poverty faced by his family, he started moving for work to earn wages. Days passed away, his elder brother and his elder sister also went work but his family couldn't survive much by believing the only source of income as farming and other agricultural works.

He was not even facilitated with good attires to wear, he went to the extent that he could be afforded with only two or three clothes a year. That situation lasted, at the same time, his family lost a supporting pillar for the source of income. That was his elder brother who went out of the village to survive alone. That made him to work twice than before to meet the survival of his family.

Also he and his family used to starve once in a day and eat either breakfast and lunch or lunch and supper, sometimes without food for a day. After a few months, his brother returned home with few new clothes and a petty of cash. He was happy for a while that his brother returned home but that didn't last longer. His brother went out of the village for survival again. Both his elder brother and elder sister were not much concerned about their family and living standard. The only bothered and most suffered member of the family was him. Days passed on, after a while, he returned home from his school with torn trouser and torn shirt, he had no other clothes to change. He was in the stage of wearing clothes with thrones instead of buttons. He managed every stuffs under poverty line but only with lots of tears and sacrifices. His brother used to return home once or twice in a year. Like wise, it was a monsoon month, the day was chilled and the village was drizzled good by a descent downpour. His brother returned home and took rest after spending few hours with family and neighbours memorably.

His mom prepared supper and everybody was invited for the special dinner to celebrate the elder son's visit to the home. Everybody gathered for the poor family's elite dinner except him. He opened the bags and made a search with a curiosity whether his brother had bought anything for him which could satisfy his penny desires. He was astonished by witnessing a colourful new t-shirt. He unpacked it and ran towards his brother, asked whether it was bought for him. Without any hesitation and brotherhood bond, his brother slapped him heavily. Immediately his entire family supported his brother and terribly scolded at him.

Mom & Dad: *"Why did you take out that T-shirt without your brother's permission?"*

(His brother added up.)

Brother **(yelled)** *: "You poor kid, you are not fit to touch my belongings."*

The quarrel settled down finally but he didn't put any words as he was helpless at that moment. By then, he went out of his home and sat down under a tree nearby alone. He sighted up the sky and spotted the moon, few seconds later his eyes expressed his soulful sorrows. After few screams, he was steady enough to think things. He first questioned himself.

"What would be the reason for that quarrel?"

"Was it my fault?"

"Is my life a cursed one?"

"Why so much struggles to a poor fellow like me?"

Then he paused for a moment and prayed "Oh God, the mighty above everything and everyone, you were the one who took me to the earth by giving birth, then why do you enjoy my sufferings?" But the poor lad was not aware that those incidents were not played by God. He was wrong at that moment by blaming the God for his sufferings but I consider that as a high faith kept over God by a poor boy. That night got over under that tree with pain in his heart and tears in his eye. The next morning, he decided to increase his working hours and decrease his schooling hours for the sake of earning. As everybody was aware of, two days later, his brother again left the village to take care of his own life. His elder sister was slightly concerned of that family. So, his sister, his mom and his dad, all three used to go for agricultural works but the only one was him who goes for petty construction works, school for education and sometimes even farming to support his family as a pillar.

He used to have few entertainments like playing outdoor games, spending time with family, roaming the streets, listening to music or some NEWS in a small tea stall nearby. He was very fond of music and sometimes, he used to sing aloud in the tea stall. He was a diehard fan of THE ACTOR, technician, director, producer, singer, dance artist, choreographer and the encyclopaedia of Indian Film Industry. He won't miss any of his films to watch and music to listen. He even travels out of his village to watch films. He was good enough at Chemistry and naturally scored more marks in Chemistry than other subjects. Also his grade 10 marks flourished good due to the presence of higher score ratio in Chemistry. So he had good interest in chemistry and was keen to know about fabrics, mixture of chemicals and about textile industry to the core, the other reasons for his interest over garments were his life without good attires and his past experience with his brother just for a single T-shirt.

"The Extreme Interests Face Extreme Sufferings."

He was keen to the core on Chemistry over basics, but due to his family and personal stages he couldn't make it happen to a large net. He went for work everyday, even during examinations and couldn't focus more on his learning from school. Two years passed away with sufferings and that was the year with his grade twelve examinations. He went for work even on those days to get daily wages, he was unable to manage the dual dumbbells. He suffered a lot and finally the exams got over. He was about to make the next phase of his life, he went work for shifted hours and made money for sustainment and savings. He made a huge saving of INR 200 with nobody's eye over it. He was abled to relax but that relaxation got over much sooner. The day with his exam results had arrived. He rushed towards his teacher and inquired about the results. By hearing the results, he was abacked and started to dream over the extreme fear of death.

"Realities Are Sometimes Hard To Digest."

As expecting the unexpected, the result was unfavourable to his life. He failed his English examination, which made him fail in his overall grade 12 examination. His father got to knew about that tragedy and instantly took a stick from a nearby pit land and started to chase behind him. His father was not aware that his son, who failed exams would never fail at extents. By watching his dad's chase over him, he made a sprint towards his home and took the INR 200 which he had saved for a couple of months. When he came out his home rapidly, his father was about to hold him up by catching his shirt's neck. Suddenly, he witnessed a bus in motion ahead. His eyes caught the name of the town where the bus was to go. He got into the bus in a fraction of second and made the journey towards his life.

He then watched the bus route board and came to know that he was yet ahead to **Tirupur** (a district in TamilNadu, India). That was the great turning point in his life and that was the call made by Nature to create changes and challenges.

The Welcoming Of The Call Made

It was nearly four hours of travel from his village to his new town. During the travel he had several thoughts over his past and future, his mental health was unstable, he had INR 200 in his pocket and had no ideas or plans to proceed forward. As long as the time went, few youngsters entered the bus happily and chattered about their trip ahead to enjoy. By hearing their conversation he made a firm decision to enjoy well with the money he had and return back home later to convince his father and continue his ordinary life.

He enjoyed well with the money he had, went outings, watched films, ate well at restaurants, those days were the happiest ones in his life. He felt that he had made those days as an youngster but it was made without any proper knowledge and proper guidance. He had spent all those minimal savings in a surplus manner, he was not even aware of isolating some money for the bus tickets to return back home. The entire money he had had leached away, he was not blessed at least with a dime at any chance.

There were no clothes to change, no money to buy new clothes and ultimately no food to eat and no place to stay. He had starved for three complete days and two nights. He wandered the town everywhere for a good place to stay and find a person with some humane who could afford him some food to eat. By the grace of Nature, an unknown face made his face fresher and happier. The presence was mine. I helped him by providing food to eat and clothes to wear. I enquired about his life and his family members. I was emotionally disturbed by hearing his story. Then, I gave him a place to accommodate himself. The next day, he thanked me for taking care of him for a day and left away from me as his intention was not to disturb or to give pain for me. He went away with a positive reason for his life. As he was good at basic Chemistry, he went in search for work when he starved on those three days.

The day had arrived, he went to the workplace, he sat in the waiting hall to meet the officials and secure at least a minimal job. As the workplace was a dyeing factory which was related to the textile industry, it was a good platform for him to showcase his knowledge and gain more knowledge to improve his potentiality as an employee. There was a Dyeing Master *(who takes care of the factory unit in the absence of the owner or head of the factory, sometimes even in the presence of the boss)*. The dyeing master just walked casually in front of the office room to generally check the works which were processing. Suddenly everyone who were present in that hall showed their respect towards the Master and the walk made by that man nailed him. With the sight of that inspiring moment, he was keen in getting the same respect from everyone as soon as possible, so his mind was entirely working to build his own self as a master.

As a first step towards his career, he joined as a supervisor in the **SS Textiles and Processing** factory who should make notice of all the works processing in that factory. With that good news, he came to my home as a *supervisor* and interacted with me for an hour about his job and I was glad to see him happier like that. He then left my home by providing me sweets. He never had head weight although he was the supervisor of a dyeing factory. He often gets down from his prestigious post and interact with other labourers to help them complete their tasks provided with motivation and proper guidance. He used to collect some knowledge about the chemicals and dyes, and other textile processing stages. Very specially, he gained more knowledge about the roles and responsibilities of a Dyeing Master from his colleagues.

He worked hard for days and nights. He was informed that he would be given INR 550 per month as his salary. With extreme works performed without any huge breaks, he was offered INR 550 as his first month salary by his factory owner and INR 50 as a perk. It was an huge honour for him before all his colleagues and everyone was jealous over his improvement and increment. He stiffly felt high that he was regarded with appreciations from his boss straight away. Later I met him coincidentally in the roadside. He inquired about my welfare and invited me for that dinner, he took me to a restaurant along with his colleagues and paid the bill. Then, we went to a haberdashery for purchasing attires and finally went to a film. He came to the mentality of becoming rich as everybody thinks but he enjoyed a lot and avoided to keep up some money as a saving for meeting few basic needs in case of any emergencies.

Everything went good, days positively passed. It was the date of month end and the salary for his second month was about to be credited on the next day. Dreaming of getting salary on the day next by that night, he started thinking of celebrating well as like the previous month he celebrated. It was a sight of darkness and pure silence for a glimpse, slowly his family and his cruel childhood days came to his remembrance as a nightmare. All of a sudden, he woke up with trembling fear and made few unconscious seconds. He washed his drowsy face, only then he could make few clear decisions.

He spoke with his inner conscience that his ultimate desire was to become a Dyeing Master and the cause for that desire was the need of money which was rooted due to his family situation and was watered due to his own sufferings. As a sparkling solution, he was offered with a gradual shining opportunity in his life. In order to make use of the chance, he fixed his broken mind set as a primary step. Then he firmly decided that not to spend any part of his salary anymore. With the esteemed hope of making savings from the month then onwards, he started dozing again.

The rise of Sun on the next day was a tool for his own rise in life as well. He got ready and marched ahead his work place, met his factory boss and requested that not to hand over the salary to his hands anymore and asked his boss to provide food in the canteen. His boss accepted the dealing and they both came to conclusion by which INR 100 would be caught from his salary every month and the rest INR 500 would be kept in accountancy section, he could withdraw it once in every six months. As per the agreement made, he didn't receive his salary for any external expenses and started to make huge savings. All other his colleagues encouraged him to live life as like as an oil rich Arab lives but he was aware of his realities and didn't want to believe over surplus expectations which could ruin his life out.

Few hours later, he made a telephone to his mom and dad. He dialled to the post office nearby his home in his village, introduced himself and asked the post officer to hand over the call to his mom and dad. The call was also received by his mom and dad. After knowing that their son was on the other side of the call made, without any hesitation, they both started to scold him heavily and were not ready to hear his words. Then he informed that he was well good enough and had joined for a work as a supervisor in a textile processing unit. He added words that he would be provided INR 500 as his salary every month and would make visit of them every six month in once. His parents had no hope over his words and stated all his words as a lie. He then understood that he couldn't convince his parents if he speaks more or try to make them understand the reality. If he had done that, the conversation might have definitely ended up in quarrel. So, he cut the call made.

Due to that incident occurred, his parents completely stopped thinking of him and started to live only for his elder sister and not for him or his elder brother anymore. That made him get confused, he was sitting in his office chair with an empty mind-set. He slowly started to let his tears pass away his cheeks and he was disturbed mentally for a while. Finally, he went to the state of dozing. Hours went faster, he was in sleep for nearly five hours during his work time, then suddenly a worker from that factory came to his room and woke him up in a rushed manner.

He got up quickly and inquired the reason for that worker's panic run made. That worker explained him that he failed to supervise the processes went on for the past five hours and that caused the collapse over the works those were about to be done in the factory. The duration of processing the cloth got late, if that had continued for a little more time that might have created a loss for the factory in thousands of INR. If that had happened, there would be a major role of his own self for the loss. So, that was his responsibility to look over all the events occurring in the factory. In order to prevent all those happenings, he ran towards the machineries and called the labours to fix the problem.

Even though he was not such a literate, with his past learnings from his colleagues and technical presence of mind, he himself got inside the machine and had fixed the problem. But, he thought that informing the Dyeing Master about that incident would be correct. Hearing all those issues, the Dyeing Master scolded him by pointing out his emotional imbalance and mental absence. He apologised to the Dyeing Master for those mistakes took place and left the room. Getting tensed, he went in search for the root cause of that issue. He approached for a labour assembly and made all labours get assembled. He raised questions.

"What was the problem?"

"Who was the reason for that?"

"Why did you all permit to get that happened?"

"Won't you all be cautious?"

There was a pure silence for a minute. One man from the assembled labours murmured words opposing his mistake.

Noise from crowd: *"If we were the reason for the mistake, then you are also mistaken. We both had done the same mistake, both were not cared of our works and took rest."*

Hearing such words from the assembly, he was insulted and he realised what his mistake was. As a lecture in his life, he understood what does profession mean and what makes one a professional. He then dispersed the assembly with a general warning and asked everybody not to repeat that again.

The next morning, he dressed in a formal way which could signify the sense of perfection, punctuality and profession. He changed his mind-set, attitude and was ready to introduce a new self to everyone in the factory. As of his prediction, nobody was not ready to let their eyes get distracted from him, everyone was confused and they understood that something was ready from his side to destruct mistakes and losses in that factory. He walked from the factory lawn to the office room which denoted strictness and confidence towards his profession. From that minute of his life, he decided not to take rest anymore during his work hours.

He became the only choice who could stand still for the profits and regards about to score in the entire factory. He had clearly fixed his mentality towards commercialism and wisely made a decision that he should never think about his family and emotions during work hours. At the same time, during his rest hours he avoided thinking about the factory works but he had a timeline for that decision made (till his parents getting convinced and till everything getting gently good). With the affirmation taken, he worked every day with pure dedication and extreme concentration.

Realities Recreating

He rarely thought about that incident which took place over the telephone with his parents. When sometimes he gets late to sleep, he doubts for the reason why his parents were not ready to accept his words. Then he convinces himself by accepting all mistakes were made by him, he later forgets all those incidents and maintain a pleasant day with the aim towards his successes. Every day starts with happiness, every week starts with profit and every month with good salary.

Very soon, he practised his scheduled works and soon became a professional supervisor. He was noticed by his boss once again and was considered as a standard officer to his boss. Since then, he had been a trustful officer who sacrifices even his free time to think about the welfare of factory. Gently days passed on. After his work hours, he went to sleep soon after having his supper. On a similar night, after his dinner, he was called by the security and was informed;

Security: *"Sir kindly wake up, your relatives are waiting for you outside."*

He had no idea over those words but he went out to see with some curiosity. He suspiciously saw the partial shades of them from a long sight, trying to find whom it would be. He went nearer and was abacked at seeing them. He witnessed his elder brother and an unknown girl standing nearby, he was unable to react by seeing them. He had no words to express out, was confused. He didn't know how to respond, either to act as a well wisher or to inquire the reason for their visit. Suddenly his brother holded his hands and spoke with him.

Elder Brother: *"Brother, sorry for the past incidents and kindly apologise me if I had done any mistake."*

He: *"Oh brother, it's fine. If you apologise to me then I must also ask you to forgive me if I had made any mistakes, sorry."*

Elder Brother: *"Thank God, everything is good now."*

He pulled his brother aside and questioned.

He: *"Fine. Leave all those stuffs, who's that girl standing aside?"*

Elder Brother: *"That's what actually the main reason for our visit tonight brother."*

He: *"Kindly tell me quicker in a shorter way instead of roaming around somewhere in the outer ring road."*

Elder brother: *"Yeah OK, let me come straight to the point. She is the girl whom I am yet to marry. She has believed in me and came out of her house and the same* *was I did too. Now we do have no money to meet our expenses."*

He (interrupting): *"No money! What do you mean? You had informed me and our whole family that you work in a large hotel and own lots of money, then how come....?"*

Elder Brother: *"Yeah, I told but those were just for the sake of getting respect and care from our family and neighbours whenever I return home. The reality is that I work as a server in a small time restaurant, I do not make the money as you all believe and now I have left the job too."*

Hearing all those, he was astonished and stood still upright without any reply. He couldn't tolerate all those lies told.

He: *"What are you about to do now?"*

His brother slowly approached.

Elder brother: *"Kindly help us by lending me INR 500 by which we could lead a good life ahead, please don't refuse. We both had come with a belief that you wouldn't leave our hands in any case of emergency, kindly help us."*

He was unable to take any decision, it was already 10:00 p.m. He was confused whether to ignore them or to help them by providing his one month salary. One month salary won't make a huge change in his life but that might change his brother's whole life. Finally, he decided to hand over the money his brother asked, at least for the sake of his brotherhood emotion. So, he called his boss and explained what had happened there. Without any hesitation and burden, his boss came to the spot and handed him the money. His boss didn't question him anything, that was the trust and respect his boss had on him. As per his decision made, he finally gave the money his brother asked and sent them off. After their absence, he felt so glad over the presence of his boss during that incident and felt proud as he had helped his brother to lead a good life.

"Trees Alive Raise Lives Even When They Get Hurt Or Destroyed."

Few months later, it was the time for making a visit to his village as it was a festive season. He received INR 3200 from his boss as his six month salary and started to travel. During his travel, he invited me to visit his mom & dad and spend time with him during that holiday. As he was the well known person in my life and the only bond I had in my life, I agreed to travel with him.

Few hours later, we reached his village and everybody were gathered at their home to welcome him who had arrived home after a long gap. To his surprise, his brother was also there in that home, his sister was eagerly cooking special dishes in the kitchen. His parents welcomed him and the whole day went happily. That was the first time I used to sit with a family and they all interacted with me well and treated me as their own family member. Everybody present there was happy by forgetting all their worries.

Some hours later, it was the time for dinner. Everyone had gathered for the dinner, his brother sat in the same place where he used to sit in his childhood. His childhood days came to his remembrance, especially that incident in which he was slapped by his brother. He didn't showcase any kind of attitude before his family or specially before his brother. He addressed simplicity but his mind was running by catching few literal life lessons.

"Life Is A Race, Making Money First Is Just A Step Towards Success But Making A Standard Life First Is The Actual Success."

After dinner, I spent few minutes with him and his family and went to sleep. He went to his mom & dad when they were sitting alone and spoke with them.

He: *"Why were you not ready to believe my words when I informed you that I was secured by a job, I started earning money and etc., during the phone call?"*

His mom: *"Before explaining, we firstly apologise to you."*

He: *"It's OK mom, I can understand your feelings. Tell me, did something went wrong that day? Why were you and dad so angry on the day?"*

His mom: *"Are you aware of your brother's situation?"*

He: *"Yes, I do."*

His mom: *"That was the reason. He cheated our whole family and additionally he did not focus on his life much to develop economically but married a girl now. We were aware of all his false statements only a few hours before the arrival of your call on the day. That's why..."*

He (interrupted): *Don't worry mom, anyway now he has a good life to begin. Right?"*

His mom: *"Yeah, but how would he run his family. Anyway we can't say anything here more, it was his decision to have a life like that. Would you do a favour for me my boy?"*

He: *"Sure mom."*

His mom: *"Give me a hope by promising that you will become rich as soon as possible and live a Standard Life with good family and friends."*

He promised his mom to make all those happen as per her desire. Later, his dad spoke with him when he was alone.

Dad: *"My boy, forget all your mother's drama held before few minutes. You focus for your dreams and don't let your dreams to miss at any cost and by any means of chance. Beware of your own principles and principal goals."*

Next day morning, he handed over the money 3000 INR to his mom and dad soon after getting ready to leave back to the town for survival. He told them to meet their regular expenses with that 3000 INR and informed them that once in every six months, he would be coming to his village to visit them all and hand over 3000 INR. His whole family went sorrow when we both left home again for our work. With the motivational words listened from his parents, he worked for two years in that factory and was ready to get promoted from Supervisor to the Master of a Dyeing. In order to discuss about that, he went to his boss. He was unable to express his thoughts out, after a few struggles, he told.

He: *"I would like to resign my job from this factory and join an other dyeing factory sir."*

His boss: *"Why may I ask Sir?"*

He: *"Sir I aim for the Dyeing Master post. Now I got a job offer from various factories who are ready to hire me with higher salary."*

His boss remained silent and added.

His boss: *"You may leave from Sunday sir. Until then, you kindly work here for my favour, will you?"*

He: *"Sure sir, why do you hesitate or ask me permission, just command me your order. I am ready to execute your request sir."*

His boss: *"OK, now just go and start supervising the works."*

He: *"Yes sir."*

He then came to the workplace and started to supervise. He informed about his transfer to all his friendly labours and formal officials. Everyone congratulated for his promotion. Finally that day had arrived quickly, he worked with his colleagues happily and went emotional after a few hours. He was about to miss the world which gave him a better life, in fact THE LIFE. He finally said a good bye to all his workers, friends and other colleagues. He approached his boss to inform about his quit. His boss asked him to enter the office room and took a cash of INR 3500, and handed it to him.

His boss: *"Keep this sir. INR 3000 for your salary and this extra INR 500 is a gift of mine to you. I have never seen you enjoying much after your celebration on the first month of your salary. Enjoy well with this money sir. Kindly don't hesitate to contact me in any case of needs or emergencies. Try to make visit of our factory whenever you pass across our factory."*

He emotionally hugged his boss gently and thanked him. Finally he left that factory by packing up all his goods.

By Monday morning, he had joined as the Assistant Dyeing Master in **Sun Processes**, but he proposed for the job 'Master of the Dyeing'. He was not affiliated with the job of being Master, so he was not much happier because his intention was to become a Master. He convinced himself, anyway it would be a better platform for him to practise being fit as a Master. He was then able to gain more knowledge over the Master position, he used to be the master in the absence of original one. He was even more trained well. Later, he introduced himself with all his new colleagues, he then went and met the Master. The Master was a strict and rude being one. From the day one of work, that Master started to provide him endless work to left and right, even had said some set of rules to him.

The Master asked him not to allow any works or issues to reach his table, should not be disturbed much often, used to sit simply and ask him to handle everything and deal with his every problems. The Master's motive was to make him work restlessly but what happened was, he learned things restlessly.

"Kids Study Education, Youngsters Study Experience And The Men Study Life."

He was an youngster who wanted to learn life along with basic education. He would always be keen enough to learn anything new everyday as he did in his childhood. Whenever he got spare time, he spent it with the management team to know about the condition of the factory and workers. He sometimes put orders or command the workers to complete their tasks properly as like the Master does. He even supervised all those functions of the factory which was followed by him in his previous job.

He learnt many new strategies to control the factory which was an essential skill that should be learned by a Master. He was focused in gaining knowledge over the laboratory machines, colour matching steps and processes, fabric detailing & etc., which would definitely make him as a brave Master soon. Those activities made by him were noticed by the Master and found that leaving him to utilize his spare time should be hindered, else he would grow well enough soon to catch the Master's seat, which was not good for the Master.

So, he often gave him unnecessary works and scolds for no reason. The Master didn't allow him to follow his own schedule made and algorithm of functionality. Simultaneously, he scolded heavily whenever he got chance and waited for him to make errors or blunders. Due to such traps made, he often got tensed as the Master gave him excess pressure over works but he took it as a stage of life and digested all those irritations for the sake of leading a good life in future. He was afforded with INR 5000 as his monthly salary as per the agreement made by the management. No money would be holded for food as there was no canteen in that factory, he made savings by his own way. There was no proper or a neat place to accommodate in the factory, so he was in need of moving to a rental home.

He went in search of a good home to take rest and stay. After a few searches, he found a home nearby to the factory. As he took a rental home to stay, he was not able to adjust with rest of the money, which he used to have after sending it to his parents. So, he explained that situation to his parents and they requested him to send at least INR 3000 which he had sent regularly before two years. He felt good over that idea and followed the same.

From then onwards, he started exploring the town, met new people and visited new places during the weekends. Specially on every Sunday, he tried to be cool as a cucumber but his factory Master would call him for works which was not listed in his schedule. For the first few days, he went work on Sundays without showing interest. But when days passed away, he stopped responding to the master on Sundays alone. He enjoyed well after many years of gap, made visit of his old factory, roamed the town, watched films in theatre & etc.,

At the same time, he got introduced with many new people and made friends during his exploration of the town. If the Master scolds him for his refusal over call on every Sundays, he just simply asked 'Sorry' because he understood that those were not his blunder and it was illegal as per the work schedule. So, he slowly reduced his fear over the Master's unnecessary commands and orders made.

"Seed Sow Seeds."

He often went out with his colleagues to deliver the finished and processed goods whenever he was free, apart from his work hours.

Such activities gave him a chance to get introduced and involved with many friends and groups who had contact with large factories and rich people. He expanded his friends circle from a closer one to a larger one. Days went faster, nearly one & a half year got over just like a glimpse. He then got a job offer, which had changed his life to his favour drastically. The three & half years of hard work gave him a huge and great result. He thanked God for offering him that job, which was a great opportunity to earn respect, knowledge and ultimately money. He had a firm hope towards that job opportunity, as that would exist as the perfect platform to showcase his talent, skill and knowledge. He was sure, that the job offered for him would definitely lift his living standard to the next level.

He reported to work by Monday morning and took charge as the Dyeing Master. He stiffly felt good, as his desire was fulfilled anyway. He became the Dyeing Master at the age of 22. He was given no limits to cross at any cost in the factory. His boss informed him to consider that entire factory as his own one and work with the intention to promote the bills. His boss literally left that factory to his hands and requested him to make use of it in a proper way. Those words were huge, which was very hard for him to carry, but as a worker it was his responsibility to make it happen.

He had never let his mood to swing anywhere. He was much cautious and took care of the factory like a new-born baby. The extreme dedicated works performed by him had grabbed his boss's attention by observing his brave moves, skilful talents and boldness to face issues. His boss decided that **Ruby Processes** won't meet any losses until it has the presence of him as the Master. That was the trust his boss had on his dedication and bravery. His boss used to often title him with more regards. "Master, you have the potentiality to become a boss of a factory soon. I can smell a heavy leadership quality and you manage things cool." His boss never used to ask him any questions and had never suspected on his works.

His boss started to consider him as one of his family member. It was very comfortable for him to settle down quickly in that new atmosphere. Everybody, who worked in that factory used to greet him whenever they watch him. He had never been thankful to anybody else in his life, other than his boss, because he was the man who gave him the opportunity to perform and excel as a Dyeing Master.

"The work of a worker is, to work hard that makes sure, he/she never let their higher officials to work more than their work. That ethic specializes a worker."

After a few months his boss made him a request.

Boss: *"Master would you make me a favour?"*

He: *"Yeah, sure sir."*

Boss: *"Kindly invite your parents to this town and take care of them well, because every parent has the desire to watch their son or daughter to excel in life and that would be their proudest and happiest moment."*

Hearing all those phrases, he decided to make it happen at least for the sake of respecting his boss. As a first step he went in search for a large home to stay later. He made a telephone to his parents.

He: *"Mom and dad, are you interested in coming to Tirupur?"*

His parents: *"Why do you ask it all of a sudden?"*

He: *"Your presence over here would be good and helpful for me. Also, you could feel very glad if you stay here in this town."*

His mom and dad remained silent.

He (interrupting): *"OK, take your time, anyway I would pick you all up after six months, only if you are interested to come here."*

He thought that shifting to a huge rental house, maintaining it and taking care of family expenses would be a hindrance for his savings and plans scheduled for future as his salary was only INR 6000. He could manage all those only if he drastically shrinks his cost of living but taking such decision would ruin his peacefulness. INR 6000 as a monthly income was a highly offered package which would satisfy all his desires and plans to the core, but when the expenses get thrice additionally. It would not be favourable, his intention was not to leave his parents alone or to hurt them. Very importantly, not to insult his boss by ignoring his request made. He had no other goes to reach his destination in future as per his plan. He then stopped overthinking and decided to think about it later. The next day he went work and everything went as per his programme. It was lunchtime, he informed his boss that he takes a short break to leave for a restaurant.

Boss: *"How do you go?"*

He: *"I will go by catching a bus and few steps of walk."*

His boss told him to wait for a minute and opened his drawer, took a key and handed it to him. He had no idea what to do. His boss asked him to use his own car, travel comfortably and not to suffer bad through bus by wasting time. He tried to ignore, but his boss added words. *"No cross questions. Won't you obey my words?"* Nodding his head, he accepted to use the car which his boss owned. He took it to a restaurant and parked it outside, then went in and started to have his lunch. Suddenly, a waiter approached him and asked whether the car parked outside was his one. He replied positively and asked him *"What had happened?"* He replied *"Sorry to inform you this sir. Just come with me"*. He rushed outside to know what had happened. By making a sight over the car, he was arrested by shock. The car was hit heavily by a Municipal Corporation Truck.

He went towards the truck driver with a sudden force to hold his shirt's neck. By scolding the driver to the extent, he asked to fix all those damages immediately. The driver got panicked and started to build lots of SORRIES. Few minutes later, his boss reached the spot and started to cool him down and asked him not to get tensed. His boss requested him to leave that spot and told him, not to bother about it. Then he left that spot by staring at that driver. His boss went to the factory after an hour and saw him. He was sitting in his office chair, hands over cheeks and laid his head down, carrying worries. His boss went near him and convinced him and asked to forget what had happened previously & feel free. His boss gave him 15 minutes to get ready and go back to work. As per the timeline given, he got ready and went to the work. Gently, that day got over. Next day, his boss did not show his presence in the factory. He then asked the other staffs about his boss's absence. He got to know that his boss had felt ill. Hearing that, immediately he went to his boss' home and waited in the hall for his arrival from his room. Few minutes later, his boss' brother-in-law came.

Brother-in-law: *"Master, why did you leave all the works as it is in the factory and came here?"*

He: *"Sir, I heard that my boss feels ill. So I came to inquire about the illness."*

Brother-in-law: *"Oh, okay. He feels better. You may leave now."*

He: *"Sure, sir. I will leave soon after making a visit over my boss."*

Brother-in-law: *"Won't you obey my order? Just do what I say. Get out now."*

His boss interrupted.

Boss: *"Why are you shouting, man? What happened? Anything serious? Oh! master, when did you come?"*

He: *"Just now, sir."*

Boss: *"Okay, anyway. Just sit in the chair and make yourself comfortable. It is like your house."*

Brother-in-law: *"Hey, get up, man."*

Boss: *"What happened? Why do you make him stand?"*

Brother-in-law: *"He had left all his works as it as in the factory and came here. But you welcome him and make him sit in the chair."*

Boss: *"Why do you raise your voice? Is it a worthy reason to shout out? As a beloved, trustable and loyal man, he came as a well-wisher to enquire about my health. How could you scold him for such a silly reason?"*

Brother-in-law: *"In fact, he was the reason for damaging our car yesterday."*

Boss: *"No, you are mistaken. It was not his fault. I was the one who forced him to use my car and, what could he do for the driver's mistake?"*

Brother-in-law: *"Stop supporting him. He is after all just a labourer, who lend his hands every month to get monthly salary from us. Don't insult me in front of this cheap man."*

Boss (yelled): *"You idiot! You are the cheapest man here. Speak with some basic sense. He is the main pillar for our economical standard. Our factory would have met several losses in case of his absence and we would be cornered by debt traps everywhere. Is this how the way you make use of a precious gem? And very importantly, I have never considered him as a labourer. He is one of my family members."*

Brother-in-law (interrupting): *That's why he has the gut to stand still here even after these quarrels going on within the family. Hey, don't you know how to behave as a labourer? If your boss always allows you to feel free, where did your senses go and don't you have some basic self-respect and set of principles to follow?"*

He: *"I do have, sir."*

Brother-in-law: *"What are you going to do with those? Oh, you are trying to catch your boss' seat by taking advantages, right? First know your limits."*

All of a sudden, his boss raised his hands over his brother-in-law and terribly shouted.

Boss*: "Who are you to ask him these questions and who gave you the rights to scold my man? If you open your mouth once again, then I won't be responsible if anything happens here. Please excuse me. Without any hesitation, I will send you out of my home. Just shut your mouth and get out from my sight."*

His brother-in-law sniffed hard, turned his face aside and went to his room. His boss scolded him and spoke out.

Boss*: "Master, kindly apologize me."*

He*: "Sir, no, please."*

Boss*: "Please don't make me feel guilty. Please forget what happened now. Please don't make notice of it. My brother-in-law came here for a holiday. He will return to his town after three days. I will warn him not to repeat it again in his life anymore to whomever it may be. Don't worry. Now you leave. Let us meet at the factory after my arrival by evening time. But for sure, today I won't leave my brother-in-law simply just like that. Within tomorrow's noon, he will apologize to you."*

He returned to the factory silently, but his mind was repeatedly thinking about that previous quarrel. By evening, his boss reached the factory with his brother-in-law. After watching them both, he stood in the office quietly. Brother-in-law came near him and spoke.

Brother-in-law: *"Master, kindly apologize me for my non sensed mistake made."*

He remained silent.

Brother-in-law: *"Kindly open your mouth and reply positively that you have forgiven me."*

He*: "Sir, it's fine. I am not such a great man to forgive or apologize anybody. I have only one request for you. Kindly make notice of not repeating such activity to anyone in life hereafter."*

Brother-in-law: *"Definitely I won't. I have realized my mistake. And now I am aware of the importance over every worker in every workplace."*

A Worker Works For His Salary And Earn Credits To Make His Boss Earn Profits By Working For Success.

He went to sleep much earlier on that night. After few minutes, he was not able to doze down. So, he spoke with his inner conscience.

"It has been several years since I started my earnings as a factory worker. It was hard for me to get promoted from a supervisor to assistant dyeing master and ultimately as a dyeing master now. I am now 25. This is the time to think about my future. What is the next step I am about to take in my life?"

After few hours, he finally took a decision to leave **Ruby Processes** after 6 months and move to another factory. The reason was to earn more and get settled in life as soon as possible. By the day next, he started applying for a job opportunity in a new and better factory which could afford him more salary as per his desire. Months passed away. So he informed his boss about his transfer.

Boss: *"I don't know the reason for your decision made but I know that any decision made by you would have a clear and brave reason behind it. But anyway, lead a happy life which is waiting for you ahead. Don't forget us all after your transfer from here to other company. Yeah, wait. You didn't inform me to which company you are transferring to. Will you?"*

He: *"Yes, sir. It's **Narmatha Dyeing**."*

Hearing that, his boss was abacked. He felt proud and happy as **Narmatha Dyeing** was one of the most reputed and successful factories in that entire town. He finally thanked his boss for giving him that great opportunity to excel as the Master of a dyeing factory which was his desire and left **Ruby Processes** with a 4 year experience as Dyeing Master of a factory. It was the most precious times of his life which had changed his life entirely. He joined as the dyeing master of Narmatha. Also he was welcomed positively into the factory.

He was offered INR 1 lakh as his salary per annum. As the salary was high, he worked to the extent. Months passed away with lots of successes and making huge profits. The cause for all those successes and profits was his smart performance as a Dyeing Master. **Narmatha Dyeing** was grown into much successful factory than before. After a year, every large factories in the town came to know about his braveness. He was the most required Dyeing Master by all other reputed factories. It was spoken outside that he was the bravest master among the factories present in his region. It was assured that no losses would be faced by a factory which had him as the Dyeing Master. Knowing all those from the industrial personalities and factory owners, his friends came to him.

Friends: *"Do you know a fact? You are now popular among the industrial icons. Every knitting owners provide loads of cloths to dyeing factories to dye them out. They provide orders by checking the capability of a Dyeing Master as a major fact. Now most of them have lots of trust over your performance to the core. So this is the right time."*

He: *"What do you insist me to do?"*

Friends: *"Let us four join together and start our own dyeing factory."*

He: *"Stop joking. Leave me to do my work."*

Friends: *"We are bit serious man."*

He started leaving that place. His friend shouted.

Friends (shouted): *"Hey listen to us. If you accept, then we may proceed forward. We would surely make an industrial revolution if we do that. Anyway, take time till tomorrow's night. Think well man."*

He finally went to his room and started to take rest. Slowly he dozed. Suddenly he heard a voice,

"After all, you are just a labour who lay down your hands every month to get salary."

With heavy breathings, he got up and turned the lights on. He went in front of the mirror and started thinking about that idea told by his friends. The next morning he called all his friends and went to a knitting factory. After making a sight of him, the knitting owner came and welcomed him into the office.

Knitting owner: "Hello sir, tell me what's the matter?"

He: "We came to receive orders from your factory to process them out."

Knitting owner: "Sir, as per the schedule, the order for your factory will be delivered in Narmatha Dyeing by tomorrow's evening. You may then process it out and hand over to the garment company."

He: "Yeah. That's fine, leave that aside, I came here to discuss about making business between us."

Knitting owner: "Couldn't catch you up sir."

He: "Sir, we four are about to start our own factory. So we approached you to take orders and make business with you. Would you join your hands with us?"

He was astonished by hearing his reply and congratulated him.

Knitting owner: "What question do you rise to me sir? By ignoring you and my friends, then to whom will I give the orders? Don't worry, I will make my complete support for your decision.

He: *"Thanks a lot sir and would you make me another favour?*

Knitting owner: *"Yeah sure. Ask without any hesitation.*

He: *"Kindly tell your friends about our new factory and let me get introduced with them to make businesses with them too."*

Knitting owner: *"Sure sir. I will and finally, All the Best sir."*

Everybody came out of that factory. His friends hugged him and they all started to celebrate by enjoying well at that moment. For the next one week, he went to all his known knittings and garment companies to gain more support. He went to his old factories i.e. **SS Textiles and Processes, Sun Processes, Ruby Processes** and asked them to support him by sending some loads of cloth which they feel they couldn't process when their factory missionaries were busy with other loads. Finally, he went to inform **Narmatha Dyeing** owner.

He: *"Sir, I wish to leave this factory."*

Boss: *"Why sir? What had happened?"*

He: *"Nothing to blame about the factory or personally you sir. It is just my own wish."*

Boss: *"Let it be. Don't I deserve to know the actual reason?"*

He: *"Definitely you do, sir."*

Boss: *"Then, tell me what?"*

He: *"Sir, actually me and my friends have decided to start our own factory. So..."*

Boss (interrupting): *"Hmm, I got it. That's a good decision. Why do you hesitate to inform me? Fine, leave it. What about the finance side? What investment plan do you have?"*

He: *"Actually, we plan to hold ownership by enacting as partners. Each of us make our investment with 2,50,000 INR to start the business. Earnings will be shared by four shares, one for each. Either it is profit or loss, it would be shared equally, 25% for each."*

Boss: *"Have you arranged the money for your investment?"*

He: *"I have asked for money from a formal source of sector."*

Boss: *"Good. Anyway, live happily. I don't want to spoil your future by asking you to stay here as a Dyeing Master forever. Go ahead man."*

Later, he was called by a garment company named **Odissi Garments** and was provided loads of cloth to process out. He thanked that company for supporting him by providing the first order to his factory with a great belief and trust over him.

He returned home and called all his friends to tell them all what had happened in the factory that day. They all were flourished with happiness. Later, they all started to think about the arrangements to be done to start their factory. First, they all discussed about the name for their factory. Many names were planted in the discussion. Few minutes later, he got an idea and decided to take the first letters of the factories where he had worked previously. He collected the data and started to unscramble them. His friends helped him with that idea. They took **S** from **SS Textiles and Processes** as the primary letter, **U** from **Sun Processes** as S was already taken before, then **R U** from **Ruby Processes** and added **T H** from **Narmatha**. They finally got a name which indicated musical rhythm(**shruthi**). The name was **Suruthi Colourrs**, shortly Termed As **SCS**, defining SuCcesS. **Colourrs** was added as a suffix to indicate the colourful chemical dyes which was the main component to run a dyeing factory.

After deciding the name, they all went to choose a spot for the construction of their factory and successfully signed the collateral documents to take the land for rent. As the next step, they went to purchase missionaries and simultaneously the construction of buildings began. It took an entire week for them to make all the formalities including the government registration processes and a crystal clear document with rules and regulations to be followed in the factory by workers. Partnership shares were properly followed. They hired staffs with verification made. The evolution began.

It was December 6, 1996. The first order was loaded into the missionaries. The dyes and chemicals were installed and the missionaries were switched on by providing power supply. The first order has been started to get processed. They all stood still and enjoyed stiffly by watching the working condition of missionaries. In fact, working of the entire factory and their life. Few hours later, their dream came true. They made their first bill. The first order was successfully completed. Everybody including labours and all other staffs started celebrating. They made a loud voice together indicating their SuCcesS. He slowly came out of the factory to look over the factory alive which breathed out for the first time. He felt proud and successful in his life. He teared in happiness soon after watching the chimneys exhaling smoke.

Days passingly, he made his first month as a businessman. For the sake of celebration, he bought a new bike with his own money. In fact, that bike was the first asset to own with his money. He used to travel everywhere with his bike with a crazy noise as it was Yamaha RX-135. A day arrived which made a change in his factory unit. One among the partners of **SCS** was interested in leaving his factory by collecting shares owned by that individual. Everybody tried to convince that partner, but finally that one partner left his company. Then, they all three worked together for a year. During the successful first year anniversary of **SCS**, they all together made a huge turnover of INR 80 lakhs. It was a large success for them and their factory name got reputed all over the textile industry icons. By days getting passed away, they all had a hope to capture the entire business field and set a trademark in the entire town. Again a partner of that company got his shares and left that factory. Simultaneously, I had an idea of joining **SCS** as one of it's partners. I went and approached him to join me as a partner of **SCS**.

Immediately, he accepted me as a business partner without any doubt over my investment or business strategies. Then we three were the partners of **SCS**. We had arranged a party to enjoy that moment in which our hands were shaken as business partners. All of a sudden, he bought a new mini car. We had never met any losses and no companies had questioned or spotted any error over our processing method. We shined for our perfection and punctuality. As days passed away, we all had an extraordinary value of surplus amount because our profit rates went to the extent. He quoted an idea to double up the profits by investing them in other businesses. That seemed to be a good idea. A meeting was arranged and we all participated in that. After several discussions, it was announced that the investment would be made in starting up an own **dyes and chemicals shop** so that we could save lots of money in purchasing dyes and chemicals, own **water transportation business** so that we could save a large amount of money because we often paid money for purchasing water. Additionally, a **transport company** to top up our incomes. As per our decision made, it was the time for the investment. But as a huge twist which was not expected by any of us, he asked both of us who were the partners of **SCS** to remain in the factory after the woto hours. We had no ideas, but we waited in the factory as per his desire.

We both were sitting outside the office and were simply speaking about having something hot and spicier for dinner as the climate was very chill and breezy. Some time later, he reached the factory. We enquired him.

Me and the other partner: *"Hey, what had happened, anything serious?"*

He*: "Actually it is a very important meeting, so let's move to the office room and discuss."*

We three went inside the office room.

He: *"Actually, I don't know how to start the conversation."*

Me and the other partner: *"Don't think a lot, just open up your idea."*

He*: "Yeah ok. Actually what do you all think about our partnership?"*

Me and the other partner: *"What is there to think about? Everything goes good right?"*

He*: "Absolutely not."*

Me and the other partner: *"Why? What happened?"*

He*: "You all know that we started this factory with the partnership count of 4. By the first month end, one of our partner went out with his own interest. But that did not make a huge change economically to our factory as I bought his shares and I own 2 shares today. So, I own half of the factory. Right?"*

Me and the other partner: *"Yeah, you are right. Now what do you want us to do?"*

He*: "I want you to do nothing but... (pointed out the other partner)You, my friend and the partner of* **SCS**, *kindly make me a deposit of your share by tomorrow."*

Me*: "What do you say? Does he keep any balance in his shares to pay?"*

He*: "Yes. It's time to open up everything."*

The other partner: *"No, please no."*

He*: "My friend, just hold back."*

Me*: "Wait. Allow him to continue."*

He **(continued):** *"Apart from my two shares, I temporarily own the third one too."*

I was abacked terribly. The thunders tore the sky drastically and started to rain heavily.

Me: *"What are you about to mean?"*

He: *"I mean that he had not invested any share of money. I was the one who paid money for him and he never worked hard but enjoyed all the profits. I tolerated all those till today's date. But I can't hold it hereafter. If I repeat it again, he would do the same when we start our new businesses. Everything has a limit, right? I remained silent for these many years for the only sake of friendship. But it's enough. It's all over now."*

The other partner: *"So, what is your decision?"*

He: *"Either pay your shares by tomorrow or you may leave the factory by providing the money which you received from the **SCS** accounts every month."*

The other partner: *"What? Are you mad? Why should I pay you for my resignation?"*

He (raised his voice): *"Beware of your words, my friend."*

The other partner: *"Okay, I do. But what proof do you have to accuse me? It is detailed that I own one-fourth of the company share. Then how could you address that you invested for me?"*

He: *"Don't act too smart. It is also detailed that I was the one who had invested for you and you should return me whenever I ask my shares back."*

He threw the documents and added.

He: *"Just check through it."*

The other partner (after checking the documents): *"Look, I spell it out. I am not ready to pay you even a single INR and I won't leave this factory too. Let's see who pays the money by tomorrow."*

He: *"Sure, we may. I am ready for everything."*

Hearing their conversation, I was afraid and was not able to stop their quarrel as it went to an extent. By the next day, that other partner called few people who were the hands of richer people in the town. Nearly eight members came to the factory for threatening me along with him. I completely remained silent. But he roared like a lion and made them terrified. He made a phone call and spoke with someone. After few seconds, that opposite gang started supporting for us. That gang had put a same side goal to that partner. There were no other goes for that partner, other than paying money to exist in the factory. But we both had no ideas to accept him as one of our business partners anymore. So, we got the money and fired him from the factory.

It was the final year of 20th century and for me to last as a business partner of **SCS**. I got older and I was aged 50 by that year. I was not able to focus more over business and take risks in my life anymore. I had earned much money which could satisfy my desires in my life till end. So, I decided to sell my partnership share to an iconic personality in the textile industry who could work better than me. After a week, I spoke with the person who previously had experience in operating a dyeing factory. All the documents were ready and it was the time for signing the agreement. Suddenly, a car headed towards the farmhouse where we all were gathered. I had no idea on whom that it would be. It was him who got down from the car and marched towards me.

He: *"I heard that you are leaving from **SCS** and you sell all your shares. Is that true?"*

Me: *"Yes, it is true."*

He: *"Fine. Just give me a minute (called his driver). Take this key. Go, open the boot. You will notice two sacks. Bring them here."*

Me: *"What? What is he about to bring?"*

He: *"Don't get panicked. Just wait."*

That driver brought those two sacks and kept it before me.

He: *"Here is the money. The sacks contain INR 30 lakhs. I would like to buy your share. Are you interested in selling it to me?*

Me: *"What question is this? I am definitely ready to sell my shares to you."*

He: *"Thank you man."*

We both made our deal and shook our hands. While leaving the factory, he told me not to feel bad and never get hesitated to speak with him or to enter this factory. That was his greeting mannerism.

For the next few months, he decided to make changes in his factory map, reconstructed office and segregated separate blocks for each stage of processing. Finally, he changed the entire ambience of the factory. The factory and office, both were inside a single compound. A separate building for office was constructed apart from his factory. Later, he appointed two female Receptionists, two Dyeing Masters, two Assistant Dyeing Masters, a Personal Assistant, two Accountants, two Promoters, two Supervisors, two Drivers, ten General Workers to operate missionaries, five Lab Testing Experts, one Electrician, one Marketer, two Securities, another ten General Workers to dry the processed cloths and pack them out, five female Cleaners, two Chefs (one male and one female) and another female staffs to help in the preparation of food. Totally, 50 employees were hired In **SCS** for its **SuCcesS**

From Nowhere To Now Here

In the year 2000, he was 27. It was 4th of August, he got ready wearing formal suits, got in his new car and went to his factory. After his arrival, everybody stood up and wished him with greetings and made a great honour for him to show respect. He then went to his room, he touched the chair and gently sat in his chair by feeling the ownership. Few seconds later he saw the name board kept on the table. It was scripted as **The Proprietor.** He then majestically laid his foot over the other leg and gorgeously made a laugh and proudly told to his concise,

"I am now the boss, owner and the only Proprietor of the reputed dyeing factory in the town, SCS. From nowhere to now here."

He later improved his factory's net worth. He bought 1,50,000 litres of water from the government and owned a certain percentage of Indian waters for commercial use. He became a member of VCETP (Veerapandi Common Effluent Treatment Plant). That was one of the Asia's largest chemical water treatment plant. Enacting as a member, he could reuse the water excreted from his factory for lifetime.

He bought two commercial vehicles. Also, he bought a bus for serving his staffs by picking up and dropping them down to their desired destination. Nearly 30 to 35 staffs were accommodated inside the factory itself. He had constructed and gave them each home for each family inside his factory compound. With all those facilities, he emerged as one of the successful businessmen in the city.

He provided holidays to all his workers once in every fifteen days apart from Sundays.

He also arranged local trips for his workers once in every month. Those expenses were taken care by him and not removed from the salary of his workers. As he was much busy in his factory and worked for the betterment of his factory workers life, he forgot about his family. After a couple of month, he went to his village and informed his parents about all those happenings. They were the happiest parents in the world. He spent an entire day in his village to convince his parents and bring them to his town. The day next by, they all vacated their village and went to his town. His parents were awestruck by witnessing the city for first time and they cried a lot in happiness soon after their sight over his factory. Later, he was again sparked by executing the idea of starting other new businesses. He was legally permitted by the government to start his new business.

Days passingly, his parents brought a topic to him which was important for his life at the next stage. It was about his marriage. He also cooperated with his parents. They felt happier about his cooperation for his marriage. Few days later, his parents invited him for making visit of a girl to get married. They all went to make a visit of the bride. The bride's father was the President of a town nearby his village. The bride's relatives had no ideas to accept him as the bridegroom. They thought that they were richer and powerful than the bridegroom's family. Actually it was true when both family's background was compared. But the fact was, he was twice richer than the bride's father. By realizing their perception, he invited the bride's family to his factory.

Bride's father: *"What do you say? Do you own a factory? But we heard that you work in a factory. Which one do we need to believe?"*

He: *"You will have a clear cut idea when you come to my town and make a visit of my factory."*

He gave them a visiting card of his own self and told them to contact him whenever they reach his town. Then he and his family members went to his town by leaving the bride's home.

On the next Sunday, the bride's family went to his factory and they were asked by a receptionist to wait in the waiting hall. They started to look around the factory setup and they were amazed to the extent. They came to know about his fame among the richer personalities in the town.

They witnessed **1117** descripted in the number plates of every vehicle parked in the parking slot. They wondered on that sight made by them. They called one of a worker who was working there and enquired about that whether it was a numerology.

Worker*: "Not exactly, but my boss' first vehicle was Yamaha RX-135 and its registered number was **1117**. He liked it very much. From then, he buys each in every vehicle by paying additional fee for that fancy number **1117**. That is the reason why every vehicle's number is **1117**.*

Bride's father: *"How come that's possible?"*

Worker: *"One of his influenced worker in the government vehicle register office used to call him whenever a new number plate for vehicles is generated by the government with varied alphabets but same numerical value - **1117**. Just for the sake of grabbing that number, he used to buy new vehicles. That's the love he has over the number **1117**."*

Only then they realized, if he shows much love just for a number, he would definitely take care of his future wife as like as a precious diamond. And soon after realizing that nearly 60 workers work in his factory & he is in the position of guarding the lives of 60 families, they firmly made a decision, not to miss him as their bridegroom. They went inside the office room.

Bride's father: *"We are ready to get our daughter married to you."*

He*: "Yeah, okay. I am ready to marry her."*

Bride's father*:* *"But, my daughter had just now completed her higher studies. She wishes to get married after getting graduated in college, but you don't mind it. She will forget it if she is married.*

He (interrupting)*:* *"No, you are mistaken. I will allow her to get graduated after marriage. Actually, I was not a graduated literate. At least my wife can fulfil her dream of becoming a graduate. I will make her a graduate."*

Bride's father: *"Very happy to hear these words from you. My daughter must be blessed to have a man like you as her life partner."*

He*:* *"Thank you."*

They then went back to their town to inform the good news to all their relatives, especially their daughter. Hearing that, the bride also accepted for the marriage. Everything was done. Both families started to engage themselves busy in making arrangements for the marriage event. In order to celebrate his marriage, he booked a new sedan car.

Along with his marriage preparations, in the year 2001, he started his new Dyes and Chemicals shop, Transport Company and a Garment Exporting company instead of water supplying business as he had already owned 1,50,000 litres of water.

He printed posters, banners, pamphlets, visiting cards, etc. for promoting his business in the market. Finally, it was 8th of June, he started all his businesses and made money like water in sea. He was tagged as one of the richest personality in his industry. He was identified even by an unknown face in his industrial locality when people termed out his factory's name. The name was **Suruthi Group of Companies.**

By 23rd of August, 2001, they both got married in the bride's town. Many Ministers, MLAs, rich men and women, reputed industrial icons attended his marriage function. The whole town was awestruck by watching such a grand wedding. By 8th of July, 2002, a boy baby was born. In order to celebrate that most important event, he bought a new land, constructed 5 rental houses and registered it on that newborn baby's name. The monthly rents were collected by his wife. Days passed positively. One bad night, he received a phone call from his factory.

Factory employee (through call): "Hello, sir. Try to report the hospital immediately."

He: "Why? What had happened?"

Factory employee: "One of the machinery operator of our factory is now serious."

He: "What? What did you tell? Kindly explain me what is going on there."

Factory employee: "Sir, one of our factory worker kept his hand inside the machinery. Unfortunately, the machine had cut his hand and due to more loss of blood, he is in death bed now."

He (cuts the call): "Ok. Wait, wait. I will be there in 10 minutes."

He hurriedly got ready and rushed towards the hospital, but within his arrival, that injured worker went no more. He was not aware of that. He went to the hospital and searched for his factory workers. He noticed a group of members screaming. He went near them, he spotted his factory workers and enquired them what had happened.

Factory employees: "The injured worker went no more, sir."

Hearing that reply, his soul went out of his body and was stunned. The family members of that dead worker approached him by screaming.

Family members: "Sir, look what had happened. We lost our son. There is nobody to look after our family. What will we do hereafter? It would be better if me and my family gets suicide, right sir?"

Hearing that, he started to scream heavily by holding their hands and convinced them.

He: *"Please don't repeat those words again. I can understand your situation. Don't worry. I am also your son. Am I not there to look after my family? Don't worry. I am there for you all."*

Everybody went emotional. He later fixed a target to never repeat that kind of disaster anymore, so he updated the machineries which lessened risky jobs for the workers. By months getting passed away rapidly, his factory flourished with extraordinary profits and he produced a turnover of INR 2 crore per annum. So, he and his wife decided to build a new house for their accommodation. As they had decided to move from a rental house to their own new home, they were much concerned on the designing and artworks of their home. In the year 2004, their home was the fourth home to be built in his street and the most modern facilitated home in his locality. People wondered by watching his home whenever they cross it because it was built in the theme of a resort with pillars, stones, garden etc.

Every year, he used to buy any kind of asset and own them. For the next three years, he bought many commercial vehicles and a new sedan car for his personal use. Also, he bought a new land, built a house in his village and provided it to his elder sister. He owned a cattle farm. He even gave that farm to his sister's family for their survival in village. In the year 2007, another boy baby was born for him and his wife. After hearing that good news, his father-in-law shouted aloud and enjoyed that moment. In order to celebrate that moment, he and his wife decided to buy a new land and increase their wealth. He bought a new lengthy land for two and a half acres. He made a small mistake in that purchase. The land he bought was located very close to a stream. He had two ideas, either starting up another dyeing factory in that land or shifting his existing factory from rental land to his new own land. But, that would cost about his turnover made in half a year. Because shifting all those machineries including lab machines, boiler, winch etc. was too hard and would have costed in lakhs and lakhs of INR if he did it. Thinking of all those factors, he postponed that plan and started to think for other developments to be done.

One rainy day, he casually went to see his new land. He noticed a thing. One of the corners of that land started to dissolve. He immediately realized that leaving the land without constructing a barrier between that stream and his land would definitely swallow his land when a heavy rain pours or that stream overflows. So, he was in need of constructing it instantly, but that would cost nearly 25 lakhs, he did not have that required money, there were no other goes to save his land except making that required money as soon as possible. So, he got debt from an informal source of sector within two days. From the next day, the construction work was started to protect his land from any destruction and it was constructed within a week. After a couple of months, that river overflowed as per his prediction, but his land was not affected. Even a single hand of sand was not dissolved. He felt relaxed.

He often went to Malaysia, Thailand, Singapore, Vietnam for expanding his network, imports and exports of goods, and for tourism. By getting introduced with many industrial icons, he learnt a lot of useful tips to develop his factory to the next level. He introduced the usage of fax machinery, purchased a premium package for mobile network, which he personally requested the mobile network office to proceed forward. He purchased a set of mobile numbers from 0 to 9 (936******0, 936******1, etc.). He became an expert in the field of banking, credits, debits, etc. He had excess knowledge over all banking departments and functions. His factory emerged as the most professional factory in his region. Following his enormous victory and tremendous evolution, many new dyeing factories were started up with his same factory's name **Suruthi Colourrs.**

One late night, he received a phone call from his elder brother-in-law. He picked up the call and heard his elder brother-in-law screaming.

He: "What happened? Why do you cry much?"

His brother-in-law: "I was asked to complete a project by tomorrow and I want to write an exam tomorrow to receive my graduation certificate from my college."

He: "Fine, but why do you cry for it?

His brother-in-law: "I have not completed that project and have not prepared for tomorrow's examination too. Everything is over. My life is gone. I took some jewels from my home and came out of my town. I am going to get suicided."

He: "No, no, no. Just wait. Don't behave like a stupid. I am there for you. Don't worry. Everything will be alright. Are your mom and dad aware of this?"

His brother-in-law: *"No."*

He*: "Fine, leave it. You find any star hotel nearby and make me a call."*

His brother-in-law: *"Why? "*

He*: "Just do what I say. It's everything for your safety. Please understand."*

Quarter an hour later, he again received a call from his brother-in-law.

His brother-in-law: *"I came to a star hotel nearby. What should I do now?"*

He: *"Hand over the phone call to the receptionist."*

Receptionist: *"Welcome, sir. How may I help you?"*

He: *"I am the proprietor of **SCS** in Tirupur. I have come to your hotel for many meetings, parties and accommodation purposes. One of your office staffs would definitely have my visiting card. Check through it and provide a safe room to my brother-in-law who gave you the phone now. I will make payment by any mode within 10 minutes.*

Receptionist: *"Yeah, sure sir."*

He: *"Hand over the call to my brother-in-law."*

His Brother-in-law: *"Tell me."*

He: *"I have spoke to the receptionist. They will allot a room to you. You first keep those jewels in your room locker, refresh yourself, complete your dinner and contact me."*

His brother-in-law: *"Sure."*

He again received a call from his brother-in-law an hour later.

His brother-in-law: *"What am I to do? Leave me alone. Let me die."*

He: *"Stop it. I have made every arrangements. One of my factory employee will reach you by early morning. He will take care of everything. I have assisted him to follow my instructions. You just relax yourself. I will reach you by tomorrow's evening."*

Next day, he picked up his brother-in-law and went to the college. He met the Principal and made some commercial favours for that Principal. Then the Principal permitted another boy to write the examination instead of his brother-in-law and submitted a fake project. He felt guilty and he knew that he was wrong to the core. But there were no other goes to save one's life. Later on his brother-in-law was graduated and was offered by a job as a software engineer. His brother-in-law hugged him and thanked him. He advised his brother-in-law to face every problem in life and never take such a decision by any chance.

The End Of A Beginning

In the year 2011, he had an idea of investing money to replace outdated missionaries with modern soft flow missionaries. The cost of instalment by replacing was higher than usual. He invested INR 75 lakhs for his betterment in business. He got INR 55 lakhs as loan from a formal sector and the rest INR 20 lakhs was invested from his savings made. He had savings at zero balance. He completely had belief over his investment. But that was the greatest disaster and the worst mistake made by him. The investment was made successfully for a failure. Soon after his investment, a week later, the government announced:

All dyeing factories and bleaching factories in Tirupur must be shut in order to prevent pollution.

He went mad after reading that article in newspapers, hearing it from news radios, FM's and televisions. Every industries in the town went in confusion. He would have not been affected if he had not invested in business during that peculiar period of time. He went to government officials and enquired about that article. He maintained a clear cut certificate provided by Pollution Board which stated about his factory positively. He had never let the polluted water to flow in rivers or other water bodies.

He: *"I am a member of VCETP. I do pay lakhs of money every month to the treatment plant for treating the water polluted by my factory. I recycle it and reuse it for commercial usage. All my records are clear. Why should I close my dyeing factory?"*

Officials: *"Sir, as per the government record, allowing dyeing factories to process textile orders causes pollution."*

He: *"Oh man, you are absolutely right. But, those pollutions were made by the factories which do not follow the government rules and regulations. Not only me, but many of the organized factories strictly follow all the government norms and do not cause any pollution. Sir, please try to understand. Very recently, I have invested lakhs and lakhs of money in this business. If this situation lasts, many of the industrial icons including me would be lost."*

Officials: *"We understand your situation, sir. But we are extremely sorry for it. It is not in our hands. It was the order passed by the government."*

He sadly returned his office with no money in his pockets. He went to the extreme chaos. I once again saw him as the small boy who was cornered and helpless at his childhood days. I could not accept him again struggling in life, so I invited him to my home the next day. As a good response, he came to my home.

Me: *"Don't worry my boy, I came to know about your situation the day before only. That's why I asked you to come here to talk openly."*

He: *"Yeah, I want it to happen. My mind is corrupted with chaos. I have no ideas to proceed forward."*

Me: *"It's okay, don't worry. I am the one who knows completely about you, both your strengths and weaknesses. Now you are weak. Feel free to relax in my home tonight."*

Later, we both talked for a while with wine in our hands. After an hour, he went to bed. By the next morning, he got ready to leave my home. I noticed a better face.

Me: *"What decision have you taken?"*

He: *"They announced that dyeing factories should be closed only in Tirupur, right?"*

Me: *"Yes, you are right."*

He: *"I am going to shift my factory to a nearby town."*

Me: *"What? Are you serious?"*

He: *"Yeah, I do. I took this decision with a clear mind-set."*

Me: *"Are you going to leave this city with your family and get settled in the town nearby?"*

He: *"What stupid doubt is this? Why should I leave **MY** town? My life started here and for sure my life will end here. My soul always belongs to Tirupur. This is my hometown. I go to other town just for earning but I am* *sure in one fact. This city won't cheat me by letting me to stay in other cities or towns for more time. You just wait and watch. My city will call me soon to catch my identity again."*

Me: *"You are absolutely right. It will happen for sure. Anyway, let's hope for the best."*

Later on, he planned to make visit of a land to assemble his new factory. He decided to construct buildings in the selected land and shift all the missionaries. As per his calculation, it required 1 crore INR to pay few money in advance to rent a land, shift the entire factory, make formal procedures, hire new workers and start processing the first order. He took risk over that and hindered thinking that as a hindrance. He borrowed 1 crore INR from an informal source of sector as it was in demand. It took half a month to shift his factory to that new town. He had no contacts to approach for business makings. He went to many knitting and garment companies to receive textile orders. Few industries provided him clothes to process but he was unable to produce huge turnovers and was harder for him to make profits.

The bills generated could just satisfy the cost of investment, monthly rents, electricity bill, cost of labour and other general expenses. The market was too small in that new town which was the main drawback for his minimal profits. In order to get rid of that, he went to some other knittings and garments outside the town to increase his generation of bills. In between those difficulties he often went home.

He used to go for his factory by every Monday morning and reach home by every Tuesday night. He again goes for his factory by every Wednesday morning and again go back to his home by every Thursday night. And by Friday morning he again went for his factory and by Saturday night he went back to his home and takes rest by spending time with his family in the whole Sunday. And by Monday morning, he again went for work.

It was his every week schedule. He travelled nearly 60 km from factory to home and another 60 km to reach factory from home. Due to those severe days and sleepless nights, he was affected by diabetes. Simultaneously, he could not generate bills in large values as of he did in Tirupur. Because Tirupur was the main industrial hub for textile businesses. So, he went to many small time knittings and garments which were located somewhere in hilly regions out of his state. One night, he and his driver went to a garment company located in a hilly region for delivering the processed cloth. It was around 1 a.m. They both were heading towards their destination in the top of a hill. They very often heard noises and noticed posters alerting the presence of wild animals. They reached their destination and delivered the cloth. They had a plan of staying in the garment company that night. But, he was in need of moving home to spend time with his wife and children. So, they took risk and decided to descend the hill. They started moving down.

Few minutes later, they witnessed a huge figure standing in the centre of road, blocking the way. They slowly braked the vehicle. That huge figure stared at them. It was completely dark everywhere. No vehicles passed that strange road. That entire hill was silent. They both closely observed that figure. Suddenly that figure rushed towards them by squeaking. They figured out that it was a wild elephant. Without thinking even for a while, they reversed the vehicle with full acceleration. As it was a hill, they drifted their vehicle and shifted the gear. That elephant went closer to hit them. They heavily accelerated to descend the hill by mounting up the hill and choosing other wild path to reach the foothill.

Later, they reached home safely. He informed about that incident to his wife and children. They requested him not to take risk in business anymore. But, taking risk to the core trains a business magnate. So, he never hesitated to take risks in his life. After several months, he had debt of 2 crore INR and he had no money to clear his debt values. He also had no improvement in the other businesses. He felt closing those businesses and selling those business properties could help him to settle out the formal loan he got from bank. But after the sale, he had only 30 lakh INR in his hands. As he took years to clear the formal debt, that bank asked him to pay 50 lakh INR including high interest, fines and penalties. He got trapped. He had good influence over the higher bank officials. So, he straight away went to the headquarters. As he was an expert in banking and accounts, he spoke with the head of that bank and no one could believe the result. He was provided 20 lakh INR as discount and was requested to pay only 30 lakh INR which was the actual debt amount he got from that bank. Later on, he and his family went to his father-in-law's house for a vacation.

That day went happier for the entire family. He and his father-in-law went to the terrace with a bottle of wine to speak.

His father-in-law: *"My boy, I heard that you suffer a lot in your business and you have sold all other businesses except dyeing factory. Is that true?"*

He: *"Yeah."*

His father-in-law: *"Why, my dear?"*

He: *"Uncle, I was trapped by debt value 2 crore INR. In order to clear that debt partially, I sold those businesses but there is a reason for that sale."*

His father-in-law: *"What?"*

He: *"There were no workers and due to the shifting of my factory, I could not bother more about those exceptional businesses. Leaving it to function did not give me much profits. Instead of getting some more debt to develop those businesses, selling those seemed better for me to clear some percentage of the debt which I got earlier."*

His father-in-law: *"That was a good idea. How much debt do you have now?"*

He: *"INR 1.7 crore."*

His father-in-law: *"Let me open up. I have bought many acres of land in the countryside along with Minister. I will get more than 2 crore INR if I sell it. Let me sell that and hand over INR 2 crore to you. You just settle well in your life by clearing all debts and continue your business."*

He: *"Sorry for it. Uncle, please forgive me. I am not ready to accept your offer. Why should you sell your properties for my debts? If selling properties is the only way to rescue my life from my debt, I too own lots of land. I would have sold those. Make clear of one thing. Selling off either my properties or selling your properties is not my intention."*

His father-in-law: *"Fine. I do understand. I have 30 lakh INR of hot cash now. Let me give it to you. Make use of it, either to develop your business or to clear some debts."*

He: *"Thank you. I will return it as soon as possible after clearing all the debts."*

His father-in-law: *"What are you saying? Why do you want to return? It is your money."*

He: *"No uncle. I cannot live happily if I do not return it to you. I am not ready to make you struggle for my sustainment."*

By the next morning, he and his family got ready to return home. Later, he decided to sell his rental houses to clear some large part of debt. He sold those rental houses for INR 40 lakhs. He cleared the debt amount of 70 lakhs with the money he had borrowed from his father-in-law and the money he had received from the sale.

Days passed, but there were no improvements in his business. He had his home, the land he bought in which he spent money to protect it from floods, and few assets in his village only were remaining. He never considered the assets in his village as his property. Both his home and the land were only remaining along with the factory and one crore debt. He thought of repaying the debt with his business, but his business in that new town did not shine well. The only better option to lead a peaceful life was to sell all his properties and return back to his village and work as a labourer in a primary manufacturing sector located in countryside, or else to join with his father-in-law in politics, but that would have not lasted long.

He was mentally stressed. So, he went to a powerful temple with his family in order to relax for a while. He was sparked with an idea. He took two papers and wrote. **Sell properties and return back to village** in one paper and **Continue business** in other paper. He asked his wife to fold and shuffle those two papers well.

His wife shuffled and asked him to take any one of those two papers. He closed his eyes and was about to take one of them. In between that, he received a phone call from a garment industry.

Garment employee: *"Sir, the government passed the order. Tirupur can again breathe well through dyeing factories. You may shift back your factory to Tirupur and catch your identity again. As a primary step, we provide you loads of cloth to dye and process them out. Are you interested in accepting the order, sir? (he was stunned and speechless) Sir, am I audible? Sir, sir...."*

He: *"Yeah, it is audible. Let me call you back after a while."*

He had no money to shift his factory back again to Tirupur. If he decides to shift his factory back to Tirupur, he should again borrow one crore INR from any source of sector as a debt. So, he put the burden over nature and was ready to live the life whatever he chooses from the choices. He prayed for betterment and took a paper. He then unfolded that chosen paper.

O-A-K, A-A-K

He again received a phone call from that garment company.

Garment employee: *"Sir, what have you decided?"*

He: *"Inform your boss that I have accepted your order.* ***I am coming for my crown.****"*

Garment employee (excitedly): *"Sure sir, let's do it."*

He then was confused for locating his factory in Tirupur, whether in the rental land in which he made business on the previous years or in his own land. He thought that anyway he would again shift it to his own land one day from the rental land straightaway. That would again cost about a 1 crore INR. So he wisely decided to shift his factory to his own land. As a next step, he borrowed 2 crore INR from a money lender and took affirmation not to borrow money anymore from others as debt. He spent 1 crore INR to shift his factory from the town to his own land in Tirupur. He spent other 1 crore INR to replace every missionaries with modern technology that decreased the need of workers drastically. So, he saved lots of money in salary basis every month. Also, updates made for those missionaries fastened up the processing of cloth. If he had processed 7-8 orders per week before the update, he processed 8-10 orders per week after that update. That helped him to generate more bills every month and earn more profits. He gradually improved his earnings and made turnovers in crores of INR every year. He used to have 30-50 lakhs of outdated bills every year. He repaid one third of his total debt amount within 3 years. He bought 2 new cars, one sedan and one hatchback.

Every day, he used to wake up at 4 a.m. and practice some physical games and activities. So, he went for a ground nearby his home where many rich personalities went. Likewise, he got introduced with many new friends. But the only drawback in that ground was; many unknown faces also went to that ground. Many of his friends including him felt the lack of privacy. So, he stopped moving to that ground and went to an organization assembled in his residential colony. He went to every meetings and paid money for the betterment of the colony. Many other residents also paid money like him. That was a mandatory rule in that organization. But that organization failed to keep proper records over the expenses made from the collected money. No proper elections were held but formed a worthless department which had several loopholes in the management and maintenance. He raised questions over that management team about their improper records and the worst management but they did not answer properly to his questions. So, he left that organization. Simultaneously, his industrial friends and other richer personalities called him. He and his friends invited the top 100 trustable, rich and friendly personalities of the city to form their own sports, fitness and entertainment club.

Out of 100 members and their families, the first 14 members were crowned as the Executive Committee members who were assumed as the founders of that club and they were the first investors of that club. They elected four members from that Executive Committee members as the President, the Vice President, the Secretary and the Sub-Secretary for the proper maintenance and management of the club. They announced that proper elections would be held once in every five years. They constructed the club with top modern facilities including gym, boardroom, yoga and aerobics hall, indoor and outdoor badminton courts, massage and spa centre, kids play area, special walk path around the club, some spacious land for parties, celebrations and ceremonies, trees around the entire club, outdoor dining area and a home for the security and their family. They entitled that club as **Tirupur Sports and Fitness Academy.** He bought a new SUV car for that celebration.

Many months later, he was decently flourished with profits. He thought of repaying all his debts by the year 2020 but he was unable to repay due to the pandemic year raised by COVID-19. Every businesses were temporarily shut. All the imports and exports were blocked. Every industries in the world suffered a lot. All the orders were cancelled. Many large scale industries were entirely vanished off but he lasted with the savings he had. He managed for a year with no earnings in the first wave of coronavirus. After the first lockdown, it took time for him to earn more. Within a short period of time, the second wave of coronavirus spread all over the world. All businesses were again shut. For his bad luck, he and his wife were affected by coronavirus. He could not make money. Also, he wanted to be debt free at least from the year 2022.

Every hill has a foothill and a crest. His life was a range of mountains. He stood in one of a Crest. In order to reach the highest Crest of the range of mountains, he definitely wanted to descend to the foothill and again mount for his Success.

So, he decided to sell some proportion of land from his assets. He was then completely debt-free from 2022. In order to celebrate that moment of his life, he bought a new SUV car. He and his family went for a vacation. During travel times, he often spell out his past experiences with his children. Likewise, on that vacation, he recited some recent flashbacks to his younger son as he already had told the other flashbacks. His younger son was tickled with an idea to write a book and publish. As of his son's desire, he helped his son to publish a book.

That is the book you all read today.

Life is Serendipity, just go on with flow. Handle small decisions with your own knowledge. Let it free if you plan for any huge decisions in your life, but never fail to work hard to achieve your target and enjoy your Success.

He is the man who failed losses and won profits. The name is-

Mr. Vijay

Thank you all my readers. Finally thanks to my mom, my elder brother, and MY DAD for helping me to complete the part one of this book and helping me to start the second part of this book.

Part.2: O-A-K, A-A-K

(Coming soon......)

Once A King, Always A King!

www.ingramcontent.com/pod-product-compliance
Lightning Source LLC
LaVergne TN
LVHW061525070526
838199LV00009B/379